PRESENTS

THE
IMPRESSIONISTS

Pierre-Auguste Renoir *The Dance at Bougival*

Text by
PIERRE COURTHION

Translation by
JOHN SHEPLEY

Special Limited Edition published by
Réalités USA Publications, Inc.
Horsham, Pennsylvania

CONTENTS

COLORPLATES

Library of Congress Catalog Card Number: 80-80339
International Standard Book Number: 0-916730-25-5

Published in 1980 by Réalités USA Publications, Incorporated.
Originally published by Harry N. Abrams, Inc., as part of a larger work titled IMPRESSIONISM.
All rights reserved. No part of the contents of this book may be reproduced without the written permission of the publishers.
Picture reproduction rights reserved by S.P.A.D.E.M. and A.D.A.G.P., Paris.

Printed and bound in Japan.

JAMES ABBOTT McNEILL WHISTLER (1834–1903)

Painted about 1870–75

Old Battersea Bridge: Nocturne—Blue and Gold

Oil on canvas, 26¼ × 19¾"
Tate Gallery, London

The *Old Battersea Bridge* counts among those works that I have called nocturnal Impressionism. It has a little of the enchantment of Turner, nourished by a sense of reality that Whistler could have seen in Courbet at the time of their meeting in Trouville in 1866. With that fastidious mind that was peculiarly his own, this subtle harmonizer subtitled his picture *Nocturne—Blue and Gold*. It is a fluid, fantastic, and melancholy painting. The great T-shape stands out in a ghostly way against the illumination of the sky and the boats on the Thames, while the night fog covers the river with a silvery veil.

A strange type, this Whistler. Gustave Geffroy describes him as "absolutely like one of the people he painted, all in shadow, the face and hands faintly lighted.

Small, with black hair, a white tuft at the center of his forehead." And Charles Morice recalls the arrival of this eccentric, who always wore formal dress and a high collar but without a necktie, at a deluxe hotel at the hour of tea: "Everyone was already at the table, the men in evening clothes, the ladies with bare shoulders, when all of a sudden they heard the deep growl of a tiger. All heads turned at once toward the door, but they turned back listlessly with neither fright nor amusement. 'It's Whistler,' someone said quietly, and conversation was resumed. It was indeed Whistler, impassive himself, dressed in a delightfully unusual way, and escorted by a whole entourage" ("Deux morts: Whistler et Pissarro," *Mercure de France*, April, 1904).

4

EDOUARD MANET (1832–1883)

Painted in 1862

Lola de Valence

Oil on canvas, 48³⁄₈ × 36¹⁄₄″
Museum of Impressionism, The Louvre, Paris

For its coloring, I do not think that Manet ever surpassed the richness of this painting. The dancer from the Spanish troupe that appeared at the Paris Hippodrome is depicted with an assurance, a fleshly sensuality, an art of supreme distinction. Here already is Manet's palette with its resonant blacks, its differentiated whites, its striking medley of color, its touches of cerulean blue.

This picture inspired in Baudelaire the celebrated quatrain which he subtitled *Inscription pour le tableau d'Edouard Manet:*

> *Entre tant de beautés que partout on peut voir,*
> *Je comprends bien, amis, que le Désir balance;*
> *Mais on voit scintiller en Lola de Valence*
> *Le charme inattendu d'un bijou rose et noir.*

(Among so many beauties to be seen everywhere,
I well understand, friends, how Desire oscillates;
But in Lola of Valencia you see the sparkle,
The unexpected charm of a pink and black jewel.)

As the author of *Les Fleurs du Mal* had done in poetry,

Manet demonstrated in painting a modern sensibility that had not appeared before that time. "The same horror of mythology and of ancient legend," says Armand Silvestre. "The same pursuit of strength even to the detriment of accuracy." And it is also to Silvestre, the finance inspector and writer of satirical Montmartre songs, that we owe this portrait of the painter of *Lola:* "This revolutionary—the word is not too strong—had the manners of a perfect gentleman. With his gaudy trousers, short jackets, a flat-brimmed hat set on the back of his head, and always with his impeccable suede gloves, Manet had nothing of the bohemian in him, and was in no way bohemian. He had the ways of a dandy. Blond, with a slight beard that came to a double point, he had in the extraordinary vivacity of his eyes—small, pale gray, and very sparkling eyes—in the expression of his mocking mouth—a thin-lipped mouth with irregular and uneven teeth—a strong dose of the Parisian *gamin.* Very generous and good-natured, he was openly ironical in his speech and often cruel. He always found the right words to tear and destroy at one blow" (*Au Pays du souvenir*, Paris, 1892).

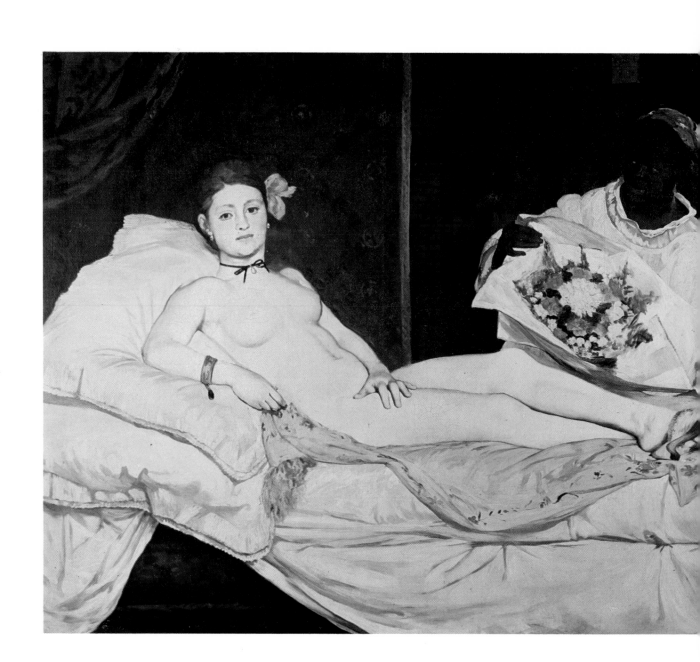

EDOUARD MANET (1832–1883)

Painted in 1863

Olympia

Oil on canvas, 51 × 73¾"
Museum of Impressionism, The Louvre, Paris

Here she is, the famous *Olympia* that aroused so much outcry at the Salon of 1865 (to protect her from the blows of canes and umbrellas, it was necessary to hang her high on the wall, from where she gazed down defiantly on the onlookers). What audacity on Manet's part to present this common little woman stretched out nude on a flowered shawl and the sheets of a hospitable bed, wearing only a slipper, a black velvet neck-ribbon, a bracelet with a locket, and a pink bow in her hair, and with a Negress bringing a bouquet from a client, and a little black cat beside her!

The critic Ernest Chesneau, a champion of Romanticism, wrote of this picture: "Manet succeeds in provoking almost scandalous laughter, which draws Salon visitors to the ludicrous creature (if I may be allowed the expression) whom he calls *Olympia*." Paul Mantz said that the outline of the figure seemed to be "drawn with soot."

"Insults rain down on me like hailstones," the painter wrote to Baudelaire, who replied from Brussels: "Do you think that you're the first man to be in this position?" and cited Wagner as one who had been ridiculed without dying of it.

As for Degas, he remarked astutely to Manet after the affair was over: "So now you're as famous as Garibaldi."

After a relentless campaign in its favor sponsored by Claude Monet, the *Olympia* was admitted by subscription in 1890 to the Luxembourg Museum. In 1907, by order of Clemenceau, then Prime Minister, it was transferred to The Louvre, transported in a simple carriage by the custodians, and hung in the Salle des Etats opposite Ingres's *Odalisque*.

WINSLOW HOMER (1836–1910)

Painted in 1866

Croquet Scene

Oil on canvas, 15⅞ × 26"
The Art Institute of Chicago

Winslow Homer, along with Thomas Eakins, is the chief American painter of the second half of the nineteenth century. Some of his pictures, such as the *Croquet Scene*, take their place with those of Manet as pre-Impressionist works.

Croquet as a subject for painting, initiated by Homer in 1865, will soon be treated by Manet and the Impressionists (Manet was to paint his *Partie de croquet* in 1871, and another in 1873; Berthe Morisot executed her sketch, *Croquet à Mézy*, in 1890).

This conception of an open-air scene, the broad style, and above all the artist's way of catching the light in pronounced brushstrokes, could not have failed to be prophetic.

Unfortunately Winslow Homer's art is uneven and inconsistent. If he shows great qualities as a young man, his talent later seems to dry up, when this most obstinate of New Englanders joined the official National Academy of Design. From then on his painting takes on a meticulous and trifling precision.

Homer began his career in Boston as a lithographer and illustrator. Moving to New York in 1862, he worked for *Harper's Weekly* and other magazines. He began to paint in 1862, and lived in Paris from 1867 to 1868. In 1884 he settled in Maine, ending his days at Prout's Neck. He painted coastal and fishing scenes, and traveled to such places as Florida, Cuba, and Nassau.

EUGÈNE BOUDIN (1824–1898)

Painted about 1872–78

Twilight over the Basin of Le Havre

Oil on canvas, 15¾ × 21⅝″
Musée du Havre

This work by Boudin is very close to the painting by Monet that gave its name to Impressionism. The technique is similar. Both pictures show almost the same punctuation of brushstrokes. Only the emphasis is different, dispersed in the Boudin over the whole picture to indicate the quais, the masts, the house chimneys, while in the Monet canvas the accent falls principally at the center, on the small boat. Another difference: Monet used much warmer colors for his sunrise.

Boudin and Monet took as their subject the port of Le Havre, where, as we know, the two painters worked together. Monet's picture is dated 1872, and Boudin's must surely fall between that time and 1878, when, in September, he wrote to Ricada, one of his admirers: "We are going to Le Havre with M. Monet." For his part, Monet always acknowledged what he owed to the older man, sixteen years his senior. "It was Boudin," he said to Marc Elder, "who initiated me. He revealed me to myself and started me on the right path."

Overleaf ▶

CLAUDE MONET (1840–1926)

Painted in 1872

Impression, Sunrise

Oil on canvas, 17¾ × 21¾"
Musée Marmottan, Paris

This painting is Turneresque with its blues and the orange of the sun. In this juxtaposition of planes and values, one divines more than one sees. But the space, the air, the atmosphere of the port of Le Havre, the reddened sky, the water, are all there. If one removes the dark accent placed on the boat, nothing remains.

The canvas was exhibited in 1874, in one of the smaller rooms of the Nadar studios on the Boulevard des Capucines in Paris. It was this painting that gave its name to Impressionism. On April 25, Louis Leroy wrote jestingly in *Le Charivari*: "Impression, I was sure of it. I also thought, since I am impressed, there must have been an impression in it." And he added: "Wallpaper in its earliest stages is still more finished than this seascape!"

Not until his last paintings, the *Waterlilies*, does Monet display again such audacity. He was reproached for not outlining the objects he painted. With regard to this, Gustave Kahn observes that "to enclose is to falsify. A color evokes countless echoes; reflections spread themselves far in a succession of ordered harmonies. What Monet calls forth wherever he sets up his easel are true symphonies" (*Mercure de France*, February 15, 1924).

Monet was Impressionism incarnate. He set everyone an example, as Boudin remarked, "by holding fast to his principles." And Renoir: "Without him, without my dear Monet who gave us all courage, we would have given up."

13

Claude Monet. 72

CLAUDE MONET (1840–1926)

Painted in 1875

The Basin at Argenteuil

Oil on canvas, 23⅝ × 31¾″
Museum of Impressionism, The Louvre, Paris

The *plein air* holds certain hazards for the painter. His camp-stool sinks into the ground, while twigs fall on his palette and the wind shakes his canvas when it does not knock it off the easel entirely.

Some figures are strolling, while others are seated. They are part of the whole in the same way as the bright patches of color mottling the path. The artist does not give them the importance he once did, when he painted the picnickers at Chailly or his wife, Camille, close up. Gustave Kahn seems to regret their gradual disappearance with the increasing maturity of the painter. But what interests Monet is light, color, nature in its daily variations, for he now takes his place as "head of this school of sunlight." Théodore Rousseau sought his inspiration outdoors and then worked in the studio. Courbet sketched in the open air but completed his work inside. Manet painted outdoors only occasionally, urged by Monet, his companion at Argenteuil.

"In two days, that is to say the day after tomorrow," Monet writes to his patron Dr. de Bellio, a Rumanian count, homeopathic physician, and friend of the Impressionists, "we must leave Argenteuil; to do that, one must pay his debts. I have been lucky enough since I saw you to raise 1,200 francs; I need only 300 francs more to pay some final bills and to arrange for our moving. Would you do me one last favor and advance me another 200 francs that I am otherwise unable to find?" (papers of the Musée Marmottan)

CLAUDE MONET (1840–1926)

Painted in 1904

Waterlily Pool

Oil on canvas, 35½ × 36¼″
Museum of Impressionism, The Louvre, Paris

On June 22, 1890, the painter wrote to Gustave Geffroy: "I have again taken up something impossible—water with grass rippling at the bottom. It's fine to look at, but it's madness to want to paint it. Oh well, I'm always getting into such things."

Monet had acquired his house at Giverny in 1890. It was in the garden of this property that he had seen these waterlilies, which attracted him by their presence amidst patches of color and reflections of the sky. The form and density of things dissolved in the play of light. To the time of his death he was to derive numerous variations from this theme. He was to paint these mirrors of water surrounding the waterlilies in harmonies of green or pink, in sunlight, and the dusk of evening.

The painting shown here is somewhat a synthesis of the others. The passage of time—in this picture where the horizon line cuts off the sky—is expressed simultaneously in the movement of the waterlilies from one side of the canvas to the other, and the movement of our gaze upward from the bottom. "Here and there, on the surface, floated, blushing like a strawberry, the scarlet heart of a lily set in a ring of white petals. Beyond these the flowers were more frequent, but paler, less glossy, more thickly seeded, more tightly folded, and disposed, by accident, in festoons so graceful that I would fancy I saw floating upon the stream . . . moss-roses in loosened garlands" (Marcel Proust, *Swann's Way*).

Later Clemenceau encouraged Monet to paint the immense panels now to be seen in the Orangerie of the Tuileries in Paris. For this the painter had a very large studio built. "I saw against the wall," Marc Elder wrote on May 8, 1922, "the large stretchers on which Claude Monet has fixed the ephemeral avowals of his waterlily pond. . . . The nails are in place, the edge taut. A strong, angry, flustered hand has torn the panel. . . . Under the table, the pile of canvases which the servants are ordered to burn" (*A Giverny chez Claude Monet*, Paris, 1924).

18

CLAUDE MONET (1840–1926)

Painted in 1878

Rue Montorgueil Decked with Flags

Oil on canvas, 24¼ × 13″
Musée des Beaux-Arts, Rouen

It was not, as is generally believed, the national holiday of July 14 that inspired this canvas by Monet, but the peace celebration held on June 30, 1878, at the opening of the Universal Exposition. For his part, Manet painted a canvas of his own on the same day, *La Rue Mosnier aux Drapeaux*, but Monet's painting is the more inspired. One can say that it is perhaps the masterpiece of Impressionism. Everything is present—the sensation, the color, the light, the proliferation of tricolor flags to which the artist has succeeded in imparting in their arrangement an extraordinarily lively rhythm. The picture is punctuated by emphatic brushstrokes, with staffs in the foreground that open the distance to the end of the street.

"He paints from afar," one of his colleagues said to the art critic Philippe Burty. Up close, the viewer sees "a mottled, intermingled, uneven, and velvety surface, like the reverse side of a Gobelins tapestry. . . . But from a distance in proper light the effect is achieved by the lines, the moderation of tones, the abundance of masses."

In that year, 1878, in a letter written from 26 Rue d'Edimbourg, Monet asks Zola to lend him two or three louis, "or even one." His wife had just given birth to a son. "You will be doing me a very great favor, for I ran around all day yesterday without being able to find a sou."

In this period, Monet was still out of favor. "He had to endure," as Geffroy says, "the gross judgments of the pretentious, the banter of the frivolous, the anger of successful painters who felt threatened, the plots that kept his work from being shown in public exhibitions."

20

CAMILLE PISSARRO (1830–1903)

Painted in 1877

Orchard with Flowering Fruit Trees, Springtime, Pontoise

Oil on canvas, 25⅝ × 31⅞″
Museum of Impressionism, The Louvre, Paris

In 1877, Camille Pissarro worked at Pontoise with Paul Cézanne, whom he persuaded to paint in the open air. Having undergone the influence of Courbet, and especially of Corot, at the beginning of his career, he exhibited this *Orchard* and twenty-one other landscapes at the third Impressionist exhibition, held in the Rue Le Peletier in April of that year.

It was at this time that he came into his own. In this peaceful rural atmosphere which he would always paint, an orchard, an apple tree, are pretexts for color. "The light radiates to the most shaded corners of his pictures," said Georges Lecomte, adding, "Working in the countryside with Cézanne, Piette, and Guillaumin, he strove to illuminate his paintings with a quiet, incorporeal brightness." It was also in the year 1877 that Pissarro began using white frames for his pictures in order to preserve the exact value of the tones.

In 1870, *père* Martin, a picture dealer who lived at the end of the Rue Laffitte, at that time the street of art dealers (he had previously sponsored Jongkind), offered some of Pissarro's canvases to the public. Théodore Duret tells us that Martin had bought these works from the artist for forty francs, and although he tried to obtain twice that amount for them, he had to come down to sixty. These paintings, in our day, are among the most prized by connoisseurs—paths bordered by trees, orchards, and snowy streets.

CAMILLE PISSARRO (1830–1903)

Painted in 1888

Ile Lacroix, Rouen—Effect of Fog

Oil on canvas, 18¼ × 21⅞"
Courtesy John G. Johnson Collection, Philadelphia

This Rouen scene, under the smog of tugboats, is from Pissarro's Neo-Impressionist period, or at any rate the one in which he adopted the Pointillist technique.

As in the case of Seurat, the new technique compelled Pissarro to work in masses and large silhouetted planes (the boat in the foreground to the left, the factory chimney in the background to the right). Nevertheless he succeeded in mastering the new system, which requires great control in the handling of pictorial space. Like Seurat and Dubois-Pillet, Pissarro here paints *where there is nothing* except sky and water to catch one's eye. Under his brush, these elements come to life, with a quivering, dazzling, and subtle clarity. We look across the expanse and the distance, delighted to see and experience what the painter has left (and is not that the essential?)—the feeling conveyed by his hand, the vibration of the light, the muted yet silvery overlaying of color.

There is a feeling of vastness in the painting, increased by the tiny figures of the two men on the deck of the moored boat.

CAMILLE PISSARRO (1830–1903)

Painted in 1898

Place du Théâtre Français, Paris

Oil on canvas, 28¾ × 36¼"
The Minneapolis Institute of Arts

After 1897, in order to spare his eyesight which could no longer withstand working in the open air, Pissarro painted a series of Paris scenes. For this he rented rooms. It was from a window at the corner of the Rue Drouot that he painted the Boulevard Montmartre. From Mme Rolland's house in the Place Dauphine, he did numerous views of the Pont Neuf. In the apartment where he was to end his days, on the Boulevard Morland, he painted the Quai Henri IV. In the meantime, in 1898, he rented a room at the Palais Royal. On February 11 of that year, Signac notes in his journal: "Went to see *père* Pissarro at the Hôtel du Louvre, where he has installed himself to paint the Avenue de l'Opéra and the Place du Théâtre Français from the windows. . . . He is more hearty than ever, works with enthusiasm and talks heatedly about the [Dreyfus] case."

The delicate tones of this canvas evoke the life of the square, with its fountain by Hittorf, its congestion of carriages, throngs of passersby, and a few rather sickly trees.

He spent his days painting, awaiting the hour to meet his friends at the café, where, according to Gustave Kahn, "he always ordered a cold grog, then filled his glass with water and left the decanter of alcohol untouched. It was his elegant and exacting way of ordering a glass of water, for which the cafés did not charge, and thus paying for the privilege of sitting there."

26

CAMILLE PISSARRO (1830–1903)

Painted in 1901

Fenaison à Eragny (Haymaking at Eragny)

Oil on canvas, 21¼ × 25⅝″
The National Gallery of Canada, Ottawa

In 1885, Pissarro settled for good at Eragny-sur-Epte, not far from Gisors. No one after Millet has felt such contact with the earth and its living growth. But he was more rustic than bucolic. Where Millet's attachment to the earth had been a little too generalized, his art a kind of pictorial sermon on country life, Pissarro—who owed much to him—was its true painter, more direct, more intimate, more real.

Pissarro probably painted this scene of peasant life in the summer of 1901 (he was at Eragny until July 19, before going to Dieppe). Everything is part of the atmosphere in this picture—the fields, the trees, the harvesters. The air enfolds these figures who partake of their surroundings and merge with the setting. All this is in a light palette, the color of honey, with tones of green and blue. The scene quivers with life and light. The woman at the right, in blue blouse and brown apron, her profile subtly delineated by the sunlight, stands motionless as a caryatid, watching her companions as they rake.

This picture is one of the most representative works of the artist to whom Cézanne owed his true initiation into painting. We pause over it for a long time, feeling the heat of a summer day, the vibration of the light, the wholesome joy of the open air.

28

PAUL CÉZANNE (1839–1906)

Painted about 1873

A Modern Olympia

Oil on canvas, $18\frac{1}{8} \times 21\frac{5}{8}''$
Museum of Impressionism, The Louvre, Paris

At this time Cézanne, in his erotic fantasy, sought inspiration from the Venetians. He had painted the *Orgy* some years previously. In this *Olympia* where he has deliberately taken up Manet's theme to lend it an interpretation of his own, the painter from Aix for the first time declares himself a realist. One thinks of the closing lines of Flaubert's *Education sentimentale*, which Cézanne had read with great interest.

This picture, of which there exists an earlier version, was shown in Paris at the first Impressionist exhibition, held in the Nadar studios. It was painted at Auvers-sur-Oise, at the home of Dr. Gachet, whose son Paul has related its genesis. One day Dr. Gachet was speaking of Manet's *Olympia*, with such open admiration that Cézanne's self-esteem was piqued. He took up a canvas, and almost at once dashed off *A Modern Olympia* in all its fresh brilliance (Paul Gachet, *Deux Amis des Impressionnistes: Le Docteur Gachet et Murer*, Paris, 1956).

It is a baroque work in which Cézanne's blue-green palette is only suggested. He was only thirty-four years old. Having left Aix, like Zola, for the conquest of Paris, and ridding himself of all orthodox standards, he was, says Paul Gachet, "animated by a stubborn will to succeed. Unwilling to accept at any price the bourgeois life offered him by his banker father, he preferred a hard existence with Hortense Fiquet and their child at Auvers, where he arrived with a bundle of cheap unprimed cardboard and a few pieces of badly sized canvas, following the economical practices of Guillaumin (which by no means excluded a piece of very good canvas once in a while, such as for the *Maison du pendu* and *A Modern Olympia*)." Cézanne at this time wore a workingman's red belt to hold up his trousers. Another of his companions at Auvers was Camille Pissarro, with whom he painted in the surrounding countryside, and especially at Pontoise. It was Pissarro who lightened his palette and introduced him to the division of tones.

PAUL CÉZANNE (1839–1906)

Painted about 1879–80

The Bridge at Maincy

Oil on canvas, 23 × 28½″
Museum of Impressionism, The Louvre, Paris

Here there is incomparable freshness, a marvelous symphony of greens on the calm and sparkling waters, with the arches of white stone joined by the wooden footbridge. The sky, the pink house, the two nearly vertical tree trunks placed forward to open the space behind—everything in this picture combines to make it an unforgettable work. It is no longer a *corner* or a *piece* of nature, it is nature whole, seen through the artist's temperament. The painter has here become a transcendental poet.

Through form and color, Cézanne opens to our vision a new universe that goes far beyond the mere subject. Our eyes are drawn into a realm where we would like to be, where all is clean and pure, a refuge from the outer world. It is—despite some debts to Courbet and the Realists—a state of being, a profound sentiment, surpassing the thing represented. One recalls Baudelaire's admirable remark in his introduction to his translation of the stories of Edgar Allan Poe, the *Nouvelles Histoires Extraordinaires*—he speaks of the emotion induced by certain works which are "the testimony of an irritated melancholy, of a prostration of the nerves, of a nature exiled in the imperfect, and which would like to seize on this earth a revealed paradise."

In this picture, Cézanne has truly succeeded in "redoing Poussin on the basis of nature." His creative spirit bursts forth in color, which becomes his consolation, his everything. Before entering Victor Chocquet's collection, the work passed through the hands of *père* Tanguy, the paint dealer who, alone at the time, exhibited the canvases of unsuccessful artists in his shop on the Rue Clauzel. "You went to Tanguy's as to a museum," said Emile Bernard, "to see whatever studies there were by that unknown artist living in Aix . . . the young people felt his genius, the old men the folly of paradox, the jealous talked of impotence."

At the Chocquet auction in 1899, this canvas, for which the collector had paid Cézanne 170 francs, went for 2,200 francs.

PAUL CÉZANNE (1839–1906)

Painted in 1885–86

Village of Gardanne

Oil on canvas, 36¼ × 29⅜"
The Brooklyn Museum, New York

In traveling through Provence, one has the impression of seeing everywhere the palette and touch of Cézanne. Oscar Wilde was not wrong in saying that nature imitates art.

Only a very marked personality could achieve such understanding of the character of a region and depict it with such intensity as to give the traveler the conviction that the Apennines are copied from a Corot painting, or Le Tholonet and Gardanne from a Cézanne.

Gardanne is a landscape constructed with love. Cézanne has left the canvas showing at the lower right. This gives more importance, more monumentality, to the rest. The work, predominantly green and pinkish brown, is lifted in height by its houses and trees. It is all of Provence that rises before us, like a person who would speak to us.

Geffroy quotes Renoir as saying: "It was an unforgettable sight, Cézanne at his easel, painting and looking at the landscape. He was truly alone in the world, intense, concentrated, attentive, respectful. He came back the next day and every day, redoubled his efforts, and sometimes also he went away in despair, leaving his canvas on a stone or on the grass, at the mercy of the wind, the rain, the sun, to be absorbed by the soil, the painted landscape reclaimed by the surrounding nature."

PAUL CÉZANNE (1839–1906)

Painted in 1893–95

Boy in a Red Vest

Oil on canvas, 35¼ × 28½″
Collection Mr. aud Mrs. Paul Mellon, Upperville, Va.

This is by far the finest of the series that Cézanne painted on this theme. The youth is thoughtful. The painter has put there all of his art, all the sensitivity of his eye, all his strength of color. The gesture is elegant. This painting occupies the same place for Cézanne as *Gilles* in the work of Watteau. There is great depth in the drawing, and yet everything is said with a few strokes. The red of the vest is like an untimely bloodstain on this boy still at the daydreaming age. The work achieves grandeur and deep feeling. The thick curtain is as heavy in its gray-blues as the youth is lithe.

It is an apparition, one which for some reason makes me think of the artist's appearance on the scene of the world.

What matters to Cézanne is not so much the logical imitation of the actual as the transcending of external reality. Throughout his work one feels this tension, this inner pressure that ends by draining everything with it. Values? He rejects them to replace them by color. The outline? He ignores it in order to concentrate on form in space. He would like never to finish, never to make the definitive stroke which often eludes him. From this comes his impasto and a rough texture, far from the smooth surfaces of Manet and Renoir.

ARMAND GUILLAUMIN (1841–1927)

Painted in 1873

Sunset at Ivry

Oil on canvas, 25⅝ × 31⅞"
Museum of Impressionism, The Louvre, Paris

Here we have, in the heightened tones of the landscape, a foretaste of Fauvism, as well as a first view of the factory chimneys that Van Gogh will place in the background of his canvases on a similar theme. Nothing for Guillaumin was alive enough. In his study of the eighth and last Impressionist exhibition, Henry Fèvre remarks that Guillaumin "is capable of thrusting an insolent sun in front of your eyeballs that makes you lower your lids." And the critic speaks of the painter's "frenzy of sunlight," his "congested coloring." In his work, "the grass is gilded, the shadows an intense violet" ("Etude sur le Salon de 1886 et sur l'Exposition des Impressionnistes," *Demain*, Paris, 1886).

The Impressionists were said to be seized with "violet-tomania." The reproach applies primarily to Guillaumin. And it was he whom Huysmans had in mind when, writing of the fifth Impressionist exhibition in *L'Art moderne*, he remarked that "the eye of most [of these painters] was monomaniacal; this one saw hairdresser's blue in all of nature; that one saw violet; earth, sky, water, flesh, everything in their work borders on the color of lilac and eggplant."

Sunset at Ivry was shown in the first Impressionist exhibition in 1874. Before entering The Louvre, it belonged to Dr. Gachet.

EDGAR DEGAS (1834–1917)

Painted in 1865

Woman with Chrysanthemums

Oil on canvas, 29 × 36½″
The Metropolitan Museum of Art, New York.
Bequest of Mrs. H. O. Havemeyer, 1929.
The H. O. Havemeyer Collection

Degas here revives the art of the portrait by the audacity of his composition. One cannot say which is the most important, the bouquet, the table, or the lady; it recalls the line by Alberic II on the Pompeiian palace: *"Will it be God, table, or basin?"* It hardly matters since everything in the picture has the same plastic value; all is conceived in terms of drawing, color, and harmony. The chrysanthemums with their many and lively hues bring out the neutral, yellowish tones of the portrait. The drawing is distinct, and would even be dry were it not amplified by color. It is one of the first canvases in which Degas cut off his subject by the frame in the Japanese manner, a picture seemingly not composed, since the woman might almost have sat down at the table by chance. But everything here has been thought out and arranged, even the crystal pitcher and the carelessly tossed gloves.

Here the artist is mocking, witty, Parisian (with a touch of that Neapolitan spirit that had come down to him from his forebears). As an exhortation to himself, he wrote: "Paint portraits of people in familiar and typical attitudes, and above all give their faces the same choice of expression that you give their bodies."

Degas was more of a draftsman than any other Impressionist. Along with Ingres, he might have said: *Nulla dies sine linea.* He is the linear artist of the group. He liked to reflect while making notes from nature. "To do a portrait," he said, "have the model pose on the ground floor and go upstairs to work, to accustom yourself to remembering forms and expressions, and never draw or paint immediately."

EDGAR DEGAS (1834–1917)

Drawn in 1877

Women on the Terrace of a Café

Pastel on monotype, 16½ × 23⅝″
Museum of Impressionism, The Louvre, Paris

Here, too, the presentation of the scene between the pillars of the Montmartre café has a certain daring. Degas has forcefully rendered the listlessness of these prostitutes discussing their clients' generosity or stinginess.

"Here are some women at the door of a café in the evening," wrote Georges Rivière in the first issue of the magazine *L'Impressionniste* (1877). "One taps her teeth with her fingernail, saying, 'That's not all!' Another spreads her large gloved hand on the table. In the background, the boulevard where the crowd diminishes little by little. It is an extraordinary page of history."

With this pastel, Degas abandons his smooth technique, adopting a more vigorous one in which the strokes overlap. He now achieves greater expression. Later he will catch the nude in her most private attitudes, prompting Henry Fèvre to remark: "M. Degas, with an artist's splendid shamelessness, strips bare for us the swollen, heavy, modern flesh of the public female. In the sordid bedrooms of registered houses, where they fulfill their social and utilitarian role as great collectors of love, these plump ladies wash, brush, soak, and dry themselves, in basins as wide as drinking troughs" ("Etude sur le Salon de 1886 et sur l'Exposition des Impressionnistes," *Demain*, Paris, 1886).

This pastel was shown in 1877 at the third Impressionist exposition in the Rue Le Peletier. It was afterwards part of the Caillebotte Collection.

EDGAR DEGAS (1834–1917)

Drawn about 1878

L'Etoile

Pastel, 22⅞ × 16½"
Museum of Impressionism, The Louvre, Paris

This is perhaps the most famous Degas, and one in which woman is not, as Félix Fénéon remarked, "soiled by being likened to an animal." This dancer on the stage is, on the contrary, a kind of fairy of illusion. The artist sees her "bending and pirouetting, her legs performing such difficult feats as *jetés* and *chassés*, *battements* and *entrechats*" (Roger Marx, *Maîtres d'hier et d'aujourd'hui*, Paris, 1914). Her bust is thrust forward, her arms raised in the graceful gesture of a prima ballerina; there are flowers in her hair, on her bodice, and at her waist; and everything is surrounded by a glowing haze from the footlights and the soft half-shadows of the scenery. The pastel texture gives the work the nuance and flat bril-liance of a butterfly wing.

Seven years previously, on September 30, 1871, Degas had written to the painter James Tissot in London: "I have just had, and still have, some trouble with my eyes. This happened on the riverbank at Chatou, while I was painting a watercolor in bright sunlight, and for three weeks I was unable to read or work or go out, and was terrified that I wouldn't recover."

For its color, movement, and subtlety, this pastel is, in my opinion, the best example of Degas as an Impressionist. It is also a work in which his realism reaches a level of enchantment. It was part of the Caillebotte Collection.

PIERRE-AUGUSTE RENOIR (1841–1919)

Painted in 1874

La Loge

Oil on canvas, 31 × 25"
Courtauld Institute Galleries, London

This is a marvel of femininity in its variations of pink and flesh tones. There is an enchanting harmony between the gold and the silver, the blue-blacks and the whites. Roger Marx speaks of those amber tones "which, in Renoir's pictures, give the skin a blond, velvet quality and the iridescence of mother-of-pearl."

We feel in this picture a flutter of eyelashes, a sense of breathing, a certain tremulousness, an emotion brought to the surface, that puts before our eyes that gift for life and happiness possessed by Renoir.

The flowers in the hair and on the bodice, the white gloves, the opera glasses held with such distinction, would almost make us doubt that it was a professional model, Nini Lopez, who posed for this fine creature. The man leaning back and looking through his opera glasses at the gallery is Edmond Renoir, the painter's brother.

In this same year, 1874, Renoir participated in the first Impressionist exhibition with six oils. Later when his companions boasted of the freedom that they had discovered in landscape painting, Renoir began to doubt himself. "Alas, I am a painter of figures," he wrote to Claude Monet at the end of January, 1884. Therein, however, lay his originality.

PIERRE-AUGUSTE RENOIR (1841–1919)

Painted in 1876

Dancing at the Moulin de la Galette

Oil on canvas, 51½ × 69″
Museum of Impressionism, The Louvre, Paris

It has been said that "Renoir put his contemporaries into pictures. *Dancing at the Moulin de la Galette* is one such scene, and along with the *Luncheon of the Boating Party* perhaps the most successful of all Impressionism. Certainly it owes something to Manet. But it is no longer a question, as with the painter of *La Musique aux Tuileries*, of broad luminous planes around a drawing in which the charcoal still shows in places. It is a wealth of notations taken from life, an exploding sky-rocket that has just spattered the dancers and spectators with sunlight. Form is introduced spontaneously by the brushstroke of color, by the relations of the tones, with no apparent contour.

It is, says Gustave Geffroy, "one of those complete summations of vital observation and luminous surroundings: the intoxication of the dance, the noise, the sunlight, the dust of an open-air festivity—excitement in the faces, carelessness of pose—a rhythm in which the clothing, pink, light and dark blue, black, whirls and pauses—a movement of passion, an advancing shadow, a running fire, pleasure and fatigue . . ."

The painting is a homogenous whole in which the artist has succeeded in evoking with equal facility the trees, the tables with glasses, the couples of drinkers and dancers. It has the gift of making us see, understand, and feel; it is rich in what poets have called *les correspondances*.

Most of the figures are either models or friends of the painter. Estelle, in a striped pink-and-blue dress, is seated on the bench in the foreground. Around the table are Lamy, Norbert Goeneutte, Georges Rivière; among the dancers, Gervex, Cordey, Lestringuez, Lhote. In the middle of the picture, the Spanish painter Solares y Cardenas dances with Margot.

The work formed part of the Caillebotte Collection.

PIERRE-AUGUSTE RENOIR (1841–1919)

Painted in 1879

La Fin du Déjeuner

Oil on canvas, 39 × 32¼"
Städelsches Kunstinstitut, Frankfort

Here again we have an evocation of life and the joy of living. Renoir, who admired Delacroix, adopted this observation by that forerunner of Impressionism: "Flesh does not have its true color except in the open air and especially in sunlight." And no one equals Renoir in his unforgettable manner of rendering the play of light as it filters through the leaves. His secular Venuses have nothing lascivious about them; they belong to that happy realm composed of light, color, and affection that was particularly his.

The man in the corner lights a cigarette in the presence of two women, one dressed in black, one in white. The latter, holding a glass, is Ellen Andrée, who also posed for Manet and Degas. The standing woman is another of Renoir's models. The man, happy companion of these Montmartre nymphs here shown at the Cabaret d'Olivier, is the son of a Nantes shipowner, and one of the habitués of the Café de la Nouvelle Athènes.

Renoir had no rival in his use of thin mixtures of color with oil and turpentine. Sometimes he even abused this virtuosity, which prompted Degas to say: "He puts butterflies on the canvas." Renoir often heightened his tones (especially later in his *Bathers*), saying, "This will not be accepted for another fifteen or twenty years. First it is necessary to do the painting, then for time to pass, and finally for the public to get used to such colors" (Georges Rivière, *L'Art vivant*, July 1, 1925).

50

PIERRE-AUGUSTE RENOIR (1841–1919)

Painted in 1902

La Toilette (Grande Baigneuse aux jambes croisées)

Oil on canvas, 36¼ × 28¾"
Kunsthistorisches Museum, Vienna

This *Bather*, her skin dappled with light, with her firm breasts and splendid thighs, is one of Renoir's masterpieces after 1900. The curve of the shoulders and hips, the magnificent hair, soft and abundant, the lips bursting with animal joy, the sensuality of the rounded chin, the healthy exultation of the flesh—everything here speaks of happiness and fecundity.

This goddess is animated and sustained by a sense of humanity. "*Elle est belle et ça suffit*, she is beautiful and that's enough!" Into the pain of our existence, she brings a vision of happiness without shadow, and sunlit days.

"His women," Albert Aurier remarks of Renoir's creations, "all belong to the eighteenth century." On this aspect of his style, in which he far surpasses Clodion, Renoir wrote modestly to his dealer Paul Durand-Ruel, when sending him a consignment of paintings: "They are a continuation of the eighteenth century . . . not as good." We might also note that Renoir in his sculptures is the forerunner of Maillol.

There exist several versions of this *Bather*, the theme of which was taken up time and again between 1902 and 1903.

ALFRED SISLEY (1839–1899)

Painted about 1873

Louveciennes, Heights of Marly

Oil on canvas, 15 × 18⅛″
Museum of Impressionism, The Louvre, Paris

On leaving Gleyre's studio, Sisley worked with Frédéric Bazille at Chailly, and later at Marlotte near Fontainebleau with Renoir, with whom he lodged at *mère* Anthony's. In 1865, the two companions took a boat trip down the Seine as far as Le Havre. After painting at Argenteuil, Sisley went to live in Louveciennes in 1871, where his personality began to develop after a beginning influenced by Corot.

This painting, showing a path descending between houses surrounded by gardens, is both delightful and moving. One feels the artist's infinite love of nature, his pleasure in the presence of a visual reality which for him has become almost musical. Never more than here have the brushstrokes of painting come truly closer to the notes of music. Everywhere the joy of the painter enhances his subject, pretext for a lyricism that takes the shape of a gray slate roof, the stones of a path, a proliferation of blue-green foliage. And the woman walking away into the landscape, is she not a transposition of the artist himself, who stops time to take possession of the moment?

Eugène Murer, friend of those he called "the four musketeers of Impressionism," Monet, Renoir, Pissarro, and Sisley, said of the last: "If Claude Monet had not been his friend and contemporary, he would have been the most perfect landscapist of the end of the last century. Sisley knew this, and had the weakness sometimes to show a little bitterness toward his illustrious comrade. But although of second rank, he is all the same a very great artist, full of feeling and light" (Paul Gachet, *Deux Amis des Impressionnistes: Le Docteur Gachet et Murer*, Paris, 1956).

ALFRED SISLEY (1839–1899)

Painted about 1874

Boat Races at Molesey

Oil on canvas, 24³⁄₈ × 36¼″
Museum of Impressionism, The Louvre, Paris

In this picture Sisley's technique achieves a singular freedom. It is almost with ideograms that he depicts the swiftly rowing oarsmen. His fresh, rapid, comma-shaped brushstrokes give the painting its resonance. Around the large flags billowing in the wind, he skillfully opposes the white verticals of the judges in the foreground and the spots representing strollers on the mound on the other bank to the oblique movements of the boatmen.

Of English parentage, Sisley at the age of eighteen had worked for a while in a business firm in London. It was near the capital that he painted this canvas, when, seventeen years later, he made a trip to the country of his parents' origin with Jean-Baptiste Faure, the baritone of the Opéra and friend and collector of Manet.

In this period, Sisley's paintings sold for between fifty and three hundred francs. They went still lower as time went on. But the artist persisted in sending his canvases to the official Salon, because, as he said: "If I were accepted, I think I would sell a lot." Théodore Duret helped him to find buyers. Around 1878, he found a patron in Jourde, editor of *Le Siècle*, who bought seven of his pictures (although the art critic of the paper, Castagnary, friend of Courbet and a champion of Realism, had little liking for Impressionist painting). *Boat Races at Molesey* formed part of the Caillebotte Collection.

ALFRED SISLEY (1839–1899)

Painted in 1874

Snow at Louveciennes

Oil on canvas, 21⅝ × 18⅛"
The Phillips Collection, Washington, D.C.

Sisley is above all the painter of snow effects. In this domain restricted to one season and a particular sensation, there is no one to equal him in all of painting. In seeing this flaky landscape, one is struck by the evocative quality of his art. One becomes part of this winter scene. Something more musical than painting seems to invade and envelop us like poetry.

The woman coming toward us through the snowfall, under her large umbrella, in the bluish whiteness of the snow covering the ground, is the note which makes this little symphony vibrate. By Sisley's engaging art and delightful technique, everyday nature is masked for a moment, shrouded with a white mystery.

As Paul Signac justly remarked on viewing the Sisleys exhibited at Durand-Ruel in April, 1899: "It is obvious that he was the first and foremost to divide his palette."

BERTHE MORISOT (1841–1895)

Painted in 1872

The Balcony

Oil on canvas, 23⅝ × 19⅝"
Ittleson Collection, New York

This painting shows the artist's sister, Mme Pontillon, and niece (later Mme Paul Gobilliard) on a hotel balcony in the Rue Franklin in Paris.

Here we have the charming side of this delicate, exquisitely feminine painter, whose development falls between the broad luminous compositions of Manet and the dancing strokes of Impressionism. There is a tenderness, a gift for evoking childhood and womanhood that touches the heart. From the terrace we see the Seine, across which rises the gilded cupola of the Invalides.

This woman in black looking over the city, the child clinging awkwardly to the railing of the balcony, the flowers to the right, placed there in tribute to Fantin-Latour, the evocation of the landscape (where the Eiffel Tower will not appear for another seventeen years)—everything here induces a kind of gentle reverie.

Look at the strokes on the parasol, the well-paved surface of the terrace, the profile of Mme Pontillon, the provincial lady coming to take a look at Paris. The entire scene, largely neutral in color and painted against the light, is so conceived as to bring out the details of the lighted portion and plunge us into the soft charm of this work with its delicate modulations, where the impression is conveyed more by the general atmosphere than by the style.

There is a watercolor version of this picture in the Art Institute of Chicago.

BERTHE MORISOT (1841–1895)

Painted in 1875

Eugène Manet on the Isle of Wight

Oil on canvas, 15 × 18⅛"
Private collection, France

Here is a little symphony of nuances, showing perhaps the most delicate sensitivity of any Impressionist work. The curtains are rendered in warm and cool grays, from bluish to pink, and there are the red accents of the flowers.

The man is Eugène Manet, brother of the painter. He and Berthe Morisot had been married the previous year, on December 22, 1874. Agathe Rouart-Valéry, the artist's grandniece, has said: "I do not believe that Berthe Morisot ever painted any other man but her husband, and he soon got tired of posing."

Here there is delicacy and feeling, and also a sense of openness on the quai and sea outside. Everything is marked by that "intense, almost morbid impression" of which the artist speaks in her notebooks, an "impression close to the joys and sorrows known only by the initiated."

Before her marriage, we may recall that it was through Fantin-Latour, at The Louvre, that Berthe Morisot— having been encouraged in her painting by Corot—met Edouard Manet, for whom she posed many times before marrying his brother. She was a descendant of Fragonard. Toward the end of her life, she said that the wish for fame after death seemed to her "an inordinate ambition. Mine," she added, "is limited to the desire *to set down something as it passes, oh, something, the least of things!*"

BERTHE MORISOT (1841–1895)

Painted in 1879

Young Woman in a Party Dress

Oil on canvas, 33⅞ × 20⅞"
Museum of Impressionism, The Louvre, Paris

Here one sees with what fresh sensitivity Berthe Morisot fulfilled her desire to set down the passing moment. Has not the artist said everything in this silken young woman preparing to launch herself on the dance like a human flower? Light penetrates the whole canvas, dazzling and transparent as in facets of crystal. Everything is expressed, everything is suggested by the powdered skin, the enraptured look, the bosom, the chaste line of the shoulders and arms, the refined oval of the face with the scarcely painted lips, the vague and luminous quality of the whole.

The accents are applied with consummate skill. First, those of the background, violent and slashing, make the rosy pallor of the flesh tones stand out. Those of the hair are finer and softer. Everything, including the silvery whiteness of the peonies and the pliancy of the drawing, justified the admiration of Stéphane Mallarmé, who, at the sale of Théodore Duret's collection on March 19, 1894, recommended that the State acquire this canvas for The Louvre.

The work was painted the year in which, ill after the birth of her daughter Julie, Berthe Morisot had spent the summer in Beuzeval-Houlgate. The painting was shown at the Salon des Impressionnistes, Rue des Pyramides, in 1880 (it was the group's fifth exhibition). "There are five or six lunatics there, one of them a woman," said a critic.

MARY CASSATT (1845–1926)

Painted about 1879

The Daughter of Alexander Cassatt

Oil on canvas, 33 × 24¾″
Collection Mrs. Richman Proskauer, New York

Among the Impressionists, Mary Cassatt was rather like an American fairy godmother who came to the rescue of her companions. Primarily it was she who introduced Paul Durand-Ruel, then in severe financial difficulties, to such wealthy American collectors among her friends as H. O. Havemeyer. She was a particular friend of Degas, who depicted her at The Louvre, at the Musée des Antiques (as it was then called) looking at an Etruscan tomb. "She paints as though she were making hats," he said of this woman, who was chiefly concerned with painting children.

Is there anything more tender, more suggestive of the child in its freshness, its happiness and health, than this picture of a little girl? And the strokes are delightful, with their variations of white, their cerulean blues.

Henry Fèvre called her "a good journeyman of Impressionism." Her children, open as flowers, are not little angels with halos. They are nothing less than happy children. To the insecurities, the social anxieties of the painting of a Carrière, Mary Cassatt opposes her own balanced art of a well-to-do woman at her ease.

FRÉDÉRIC BAZILLE (1841–1870)

Painted in 1869

Scène d'Eté

Oil on canvas, 62¼ × 62½"
Fogg Art Museum, Harvard University, Cambridge, Mass. Gift of M. and Mme F. Meynier de Salinelles

"A big, strong, good-looking, and very cheerful fellow, free with his money"—thus Tabarant described Bazille. He was a Protestant from the South, and highly gifted. Sometimes he helped his friends Monet and Renoir, whom he had met at Gleyre's, by letting them share his studio. Despite their efforts to dissuade him, he enlisted in the army in 1870, and was killed in the battle of Beaune-la-Rolande (Loiret).

His *Scène d'Eté*, one of the masterpieces of *plein-air* painting, is luminous with sunlight and at the same time solidly constructed, almost anticipating Seurat's *Baig-nade*. The harmony of green and blue gives a cool tone to this large canvas, for which there exist several sketches. "For the bathers—be sure to compare the value of the clear water with the grass in the sunlight," reads a note written by Bazille in a sketchbook, in reference to this scene, more in a Naturalist than a Realist vein. The landscape was painted on the banks of the Lez.

It is, along with *Monet After His Accident at the Inn in Chailly* and *The Artist's Studio, Rue de la Condamine*, one of the most successful works by this painter, dead at the age of twenty-nine.

MAX LIEBERMANN (1847–1935)

Painted in 1905

The *"Oude Vinck"* Restaurant in Leyden

Oil on canvas, 28 × 34⅝"
Kunsthaus, Zurich

Max Liebermann is the only painter in Germany who can be called an Impressionist. Corinth and Slevogt (who participated with him in the Berlin Secession of 1898) only occasionally painted pictures influenced by the French movement.

The son of a Berlin banker, Liebermann lived in Paris from 1873 to 1878, and spent his summers in Barbizon. The influence of the Manet of Rueil is very recognizable in his work. In his own country, Liebermann introduced and championed Monet and his group. In 1878, he wrote an essay on Degas, with whom he felt certain affinities, notably that of considering black as a color.

In his transition from the Realism of Courbet and the Barbizon School to the subtle nuances of the Impressionists, Liebermann painted a number of self-portraits in which he depicts himself a dry and mordant observer.

He paints this outdoor restaurant in Leyden with a clear, transparent, and careful touch, venturing in the execution those difficult patches of sunlight dear to Monet and Renoir. By the sketchy expression of his brush, the improvised appearance of his drawing, the clarity of such tones as the white and yellow, his way of opening the canvas to light and air, and of preserving an often marvelous limpidness of color, Liebermann takes his place, although tardily, among the Impressionists of the early style.

PAUL GAUGUIN (1848–1903)

Painted in 1885

The Beach at Dieppe

Oil on canvas, 28¼ × 28¼"
The Ny Carlsberg Glyptothek, Copenhagen

This picture is very clear in its color, light, and technique. But one is aware of that pursuit of the monumental toward which Gauguin was already inclined. The construction of the picture in horizontal bands under the sky with its rounded clouds is broken by the masts of the sailboats and the figures of the bathers who have waded beyond the first line of breakers.

In the foreground, the seated figures lend weight and are rendered in large silhouettes, as Seurat does in his turn.

In those of his paintings where we find the influence of Pissarro, Gauguin at this time is still an Impressionist in his love of sunlight, his freedom of technique, the freshness of his colors, and finally for a certain Japanese quality. "But," says Maurice Denis, "he aspired to read the book wherein the eternal laws of beauty are inscribed."

A fierce individualist, Gauguin nevertheless liked popular art reflecting the spirit of collectivity. And he was soon to turn toward what he called "savage design" and "barbarous color."

VINCENT VAN GOGH (1853–1890)

Painted in 1886–88

Fourteenth of July in Paris

Oil on canvas, 17¼ × 11¾"
Collection Jaeggli-Hahnloser, Winterthur, Switzerland

This is an unusual canvas in the work of Vincent van Gogh. It is Impressionistic in its rapid, brightly colored, and seemingly improvised technique, but in its use of exaggerated color it points the way toward Fauvism.

The strokes are very broad and the tones seem to suggest the three colors of the French flag, but unconsciously, in a marvelous frenzy of technique. The turbulent color and brushwork, characteristic of Van Gogh's works, has prompted Jacques-Emile Blanche to speak caustically of "pictorial Parkinsonism." I see here, on the contrary, the religious drama of Van Gogh, a man perpetually flayed who committed himself to painting as a means of salvation. This profound artist was something other than a "Flying Dutchman of Provence." He and Gauguin both lent themselves to legend, Gauguin by his Bretonized South Sea Islands, Van Gogh by his madness and the episode in which he cut off his ear with a razor. But Van Gogh is the one who seems victorious to those who can see the vision that lies beyond his painting.

This canvas shows Van Gogh attempting to turn away from the fleeting sensations of the Impressionists. One feels his effort to recover a certain conciseness.

VINCENT VAN GOGH (1853–1890)

Painted in 1889

The Starry Night

Oil on canvas, 29 × 36¼″
The Museum of Modern Art, New York. Lillie P. Bliss Bequest

This is a late work. But if little remains of an Impressionist character in its technique, there is still some in its nocturnal illumination, its truth, and its moving comprehension of nature as transcended by an exceptional temperament. This night Impressionism extends that of Whistler and of Degas. But the picture goes still further. In its blues and greens, its brilliance of golden stars, it contains the mystery of all creation.

In his presentation of Van Gogh in *Les Hommes d'aujourd'hui* (No. 390), Emile Bernard observes that "one feels sad in the presence of the cypresses, somber as magnetic lances piercing the stars; such nights strew comets in the dense ultramarine darkness."

GEORGES SEURAT (1859–1891)

Painted about 1884

The Canoe

Oil on wood, 6¼ × 10¼″
Private collection, Paris

This is surely the most Impressionist picture in all of Seurat's work. We might say that here, under the pretext of his title, the painter has tried to combine all that is transient: the fragile craft gliding swiftly on the river, the wind in the leaves, the passage of time. No other work gives such a feeling of the moment—and of a moment taken more or less at random, like a fragment detached from the whole.

In my book on Seurat, I followed De Hauke in dating this picture about 1887, but it now appears to me to be one of the works preparatory to *La Grande Jatte*, one of the landscapes of which Angrand speaks in recalling his friendship with Seurat: "Conversations at the studio and return to the Café Marengo, in the evening, after the afternoon meetings at the *brasserie . . . and we side by side before our respective canvases on the Grande Jatte. . . .* He would welcome me without pausing, without putting down his palette, hardly turning his half-closed eyes from the motif. When we were finished for the day, we crossed the Seine on a little ferry, the *Artilleur*, and came back by Courbevoie and the Rue de Levis. . . . [Seurat] pointed out—in one of our hundreds of conversations along the way—the purplish red aureole of the young trees that had just been planted on the boulevard along the river" (Letter to Lucie Cousturier, July 4, 1912, published in *La Vie*, October 1, 1936).

Overleaf ▶

GEORGES SEURAT (1859–1891)

Painted in 1883–84

Bathing at Asnières (Une Baignade)

Oil on canvas, 79 × 118½"
National Gallery, London

This is Seurat's first great picture. It is painted in flat strokes, and precise outlines are still here and there apparent. This technique, still linear at times, will disappear in the artist's next compositions, *La Grande Jatte* and *The Models*.

But already we can measure this revolutionary artist's gift for synthesis. Whatever there was in Impressionism of the fragmentary, or rather the fragmented, has completely disappeared from this broad synthesis. The artist made sketches for every detail in the picture, and put them together in this admirable composition which, against the factory background of Asnières, may be said to stand for the water, sun, and bathers of all the summers of the world.

It is sufficient to compare this symphony of blue, green, and pink to Manet's *Argenteuil* and Renoir's *Dancing at the Moulin de la Galette* to perceive at once Seurat's extraordinary contribution in the composition, his knowledge of color, and his skill in setting the scene (in which, as Meyer Schapiro has shown, he was inspired by Puvis de Chavannes). Another innovation lies in his study of the significance of line according to its direction and position in the picture. These considerations were suggested to the painter by reading a work by Humbert de Superville, published in Leyden in 1827.

GEORGES SEURAT (1859–1891)

Painted in 1884–85

A Sunday Afternoon on the Island of La Grande Jatte

Oil on canvas, 81 × 121"
The Art Institute of Chicago. Helen Birch Bartlett Collection

Everything here has its place in the composition. One would not be able to shift the smallest element in this great summer scene—a standing or seated figure, a tree, a distant vista, a blade of grass—without disarranging the whole. It is a work executed with deliberation, in which every detail has been thought out in advance. The painting gives us a general vision. The light, the colors, the transition from shadow to sunlight—everything has been admirably calculated and apportioned.

This great work, which at the time of its creation aroused violent controversy (even among the Impressionists), calls to mind these reflections by Chevreul, the chemist whose writings made a deep impression on Seurat, in his *De l'abstraction* (Dijon, 1864): "When it is a question of representing the view of a landscape or a group of figures participating in some action, whether public or private . . . the painter to be truthful can represent only a *moment* in a landscape in which light and shadow vary continually, he is obliged to choose *this moment* from among others; henceforth this moment should be considered a *veritable abstraction of the sum of the moments making up the duration of the occurrence of the scene he has chosen* as his subject. If the painter thus makes an abstraction for time, he does the same for space, especially when it is a question, for example, of a vast landscape or a large assemblage of people."

The Watering Can

Painted about 1883
Oil on wood, 9¾ × 6"
Collection Mr. and Mrs. Paul Mellon, Upperville, Va.

This is one of the studies in which, by limiting himself to the painting of a single object, a watering can, the painter demonstrated his ability to his circle of friends. The setting is the garden of Le Raincy, belonging to Chrisostôme Seurat, the painter's father; it is also the sun, the color, the heat of summer. Thus Seurat takes a detail of the kind adopted by the Impressionists before him, and isolates it in a monumental close-up.

"Seurat," says Angrand, who was often his working companion, "was truly predestined, one of the elect. He was as much a painter as anyone among the great— and this despite an artistic concept virtually limited to harmony. What a rare vision! He usually reduced his subject, a deliberately modest one to begin with, still further by eliminating all picturesque details, and then clearly and expressively re-created it by the single device of miraculously subtle nuances" (Letter to Lucie Cousturier, dated July 4, 1912, published in *La Vie*, October 1, 1936).

Even more than with Monet and his companions, the outline here is nonexistent, at least in any linear sense. It is formed by gradations, a halo of light, a proliferation of color spots. Likewise, in the drawings of that period, the pencil leaves a thin deposit around the silhouetted form but never circumscribes it with an outline.

PAUL SIGNAC (1863–1935)

Painted in 1886

Boulevard de Clichy in Paris

Oil on canvas, 18 × 25¼″
The Minneapolis Institute of Arts. Putnam Dana McMillan Bequest

Signac painted this work before becoming a systematic Divisionist. This evocation of Paris still shows complete freedom in its technique, the brushstrokes being comma-shaped rather than dots. The white and bluish tones of the snow are admirably rendered. The artist's touch seems to dance with the snowflakes.

This is the early Signac, the colorist who "decks the corners of Paris with clear light" (Arsène Alexandre). The accents are sharply pronounced in the trees and passersby.

Signac, according to Gustave Kahn, was "methodical, all ardor and impulse. His first admiration had been for Guillaumin. He adopted the theories of Seurat, whose rival he became because of his brilliant gifts as a painter. He read a good deal and was a bibliophile." It might have been advisable for him to have stayed with the conception and technique of this *Boulevard de Clichy*. A good writer and always a fine craftsman, Signac possibly abused these theories, which he was less prepared than Seurat to master and to violate when necessary.

He was one of the founders of the Société des Artistes Indépendants, which, in 1884, at the Tuileries, "opened our eyes," as de Maupassant wrote, "to all those who were attempting something new, all those working sincerely outside the old customs, seeking true color, unobserved nuances, everything that the Ecole and a misleading classical education hinders one from knowing and understanding."

MAURICE PRENDERGAST (1859–1924)

Painted in 1899

Ponte della Paglia

Oil on canvas, 28 × 23"
The Phillips Collection, Washington, D.C.

It was in 1899, during a stay of several months in Venice (a trip to Europe having been made possible thanks to the help of Mrs. Montgomery Sears of Boston), that Maurice Prendergast painted one of his most striking canvases.

The Ponte della Paglia is in the heart of Venice. Prendergast depicts it in quick, lively strokes that represent the numerous passersby. These rapid, flowing notations, sometimes crossed or rounded, with curves, circles, and ovals cut by a vertical or horizontal, are still related to Impressionism and distantly to the baroque manner of Cézanne.

Hanging in Mrs. Duncan Phillips's large drawing room outside Washington, this work has the impact of a display of fireworks.

It was on seeing the canvases that Prendergast painted in Venice that Robert Henri invited him, in 1908, to participate in the famous exhibition of The Eight, derisively dubbed the Ashcan School, which brought together the best American artists of the time.

The son of a poor family, Prendergast began to earn his living very early as a commercial artist. With the little money he was able to save, he went to Paris in 1886, and for three years worked at the Académie Julian and the Atelier Colarossi. The reputation of this independent artist was slow in coming, and this lack of recognition, as Suzanne La Follette notes in *Art in America*, is "a severe judgment of American taste during his time."

Prendergast lived the rest of his life in New York, in a studio in Washington Square, where he died in 1924.

PIERRE BONNARD (1867–1947)

Painted in 1913

Dining Room in the Country

Oil on canvas, 63 × 80"
The Minneapolis Institute of Arts

Along with the panels that he painted for the Trocadero and those that are in the home of Mme Kapferer, this is, I believe, one of Bonnard's largest works. Even when reproduced in black-and-white, one can admire its solid construction and its counterpoint of light and shadow. To see it in color is to be even more struck by its harmony.

Our eyes are enraptured on being drawn into the transposed reality created by this painter of the marvelous. Only the most consummate art can so lead the spectator's gaze from within to the outside and again within, with light and shadow balanced in perfect equilibrium.

In this painting we see all the splendor of summer. Outside, among the luminous greens, one seems to hear all the sounds of a July day; inside, an absolute silence. The palette varies from the vermilion blouse of the woman leaning inward against the light, to the more purplish reds of the tapestry. By its contrast to the rest, the mauve white of the cloth on the round table makes the painting vibrate. Even the cat on the chair has lost any anecdotal significance to become an element of this incomparable work.

The style has great freedom. It is flexible, obedient to the artist's sensibility, and adapts itself with entire ease to his intended meaning. Thus from this everyday scene—and, unlike Turner, without losing his grasp of the simple and ordinary—Bonnard was able to create a higher reality.

Pierre Bonnard. *The Hours of the Night*. 1893.
Lithograph from *Petites Scènes familières*

BIBLIOGRAPHY

ADHÉMAR, HÉLÈNE, and DREYFUS-BRUHL, MADELEINE. *Catalogue des peintures, pastels, sculptures impressionnistes du Louvre*. Paris, 1958

ALEXANDRE, ARSÈNE. *La Collection Canonne: une histoire en action de l'Impressionnisme*. Bernheim Jeune, Paris, 1930

AURIER, ALBERT. *Oeuvres posthumes*. Paris, 1893

BLANCHE, JACQUES-EMILE. *Les Arts plastiques*. Editions de France, Paris, 1931

———. *De Gauguin à la Revue Nègre*. Paris, 1928

CASSOU, JEAN. *Les Impressionnistes et leur époque*. Cercle Français d'art, Paris, 1953

COGNIAT, RAYMOND. *French Painting at the Time of the Impressionists*. Hyperion Press, New York, 1951

COQUIOT, GUSTAVE. *Les Indépendants*. J. Dardaillon, Paris, 1921

COURTHION, PIERRE. *Autour de l'Impressionnisme*. Nouvelles éditions françaises, Paris, 1964

———. *Manet*. Abrams, New York, 1961

———. *Seurat*. Abrams, New York, 1968

DENIS, MAURICE. *Du Symbolisme au Classicisme, théories.* Paris, 1949

DURANTY, EDMOND. *La Nouvelle Peinture.* Librairie E. Dentu, Paris, 1876; new edition with foreword and notes by Marcel Guérin, Floury, Paris, 1946

DURET, THÉODORE. *Critique d'avant-garde.* Charpentier, Paris, 1885

————. *Histoire des peintres Impressionnistes.* Paris, 1894; 4th ed., Floury, Paris, 1939

FÉNÉON, FÉLIX. *Les Impressionnistes en 1886.* Publications de la Vogue, Paris, 1886

————. *Oeuvres.* Gallimard, Paris, 1948

FERMIGIER, ANDRÉ. *Bonnard.* Abrams, New York, 1969

FÈVRE, HENRY. "Etude sur le Salon de 1886 et sur l'Exposition des Impressionnistes." *Demain,* Paris, 1886

FOCILLON, HENRI. *La Peinture aux XIX et XXème siècles.* H. Laurens, Paris, 1928

GEFFROY, GUSTAVE. *Histoire de l'Impressionnisme—La Vie Artistique,* 3rd Series (articles written after 1885). Paris, 1894

GOLDWATER, ROBERT. *Gauguin.* Abrams, New York, 1958

HAMANN, RICHARD. *Der Impressionismus in Leben und Kunst.* Verlag des Kunstgeschichtlichen Seminars, Marburg, 1923

————, and HERMAND, JOST. *Impressionismus.* Berlin, 1960

HERBERT, ROBERT L. *Neo-Impressionism* (catalogue). The Solomon R. Guggenheim Museum, New York, 1968

————, ed. *Neo-Impressionists and Nabis in the Collection of Arthur G. Altschul* (catalogue). Yale University, New Haven, 1965

————, and EUGENIA W. "Artists and Anarchism: Unpublished Letters of Pissarro, Signac, and Others." *Burlington Magazine,* Vol. CII, November and December, 1960

HUYSMANS, JORIS-KARL. *L'Art moderne.* Charpentier, Paris, 1883

————. *Certains.* 5th ed. Plon-Nourrit, Paris, 1908

KAHN, GUSTAVE. "Au Temps du Pointillisme." *Mercure de France,* April, 1924

KOEHLER, ERICH. *Edmond und Jules de Goncourt, die Begründer des Impressionismus.* Leipzig, 1912

LAPRADE, JACQUES DE. *L'Impressionnisme.* Aimery Somogy, Paris, 1956

LA SIZERANNE, ROBERT DE. *Questions esthétiques contemporaines.* Hachette, Paris, 1904

LECOMTE, GEORGES. *L'Art Impressionniste d'après la collection de M. Durand-Ruel.* Chammerot & Renouard, Paris, 1892

LETHÈVE, JACQUES. *Impressionnistes et Symbolistes devant la presse.* Armand Colin, Paris, 1959

LEYMARIE, JEAN. *Impressionism.* 2 vols. Skira, Geneva, 1955

MARX, ROGER. *Maîtres d'hier et d'aujourd'hui.* Calmann-Lévy, Paris, 1914

————. *Un Siècle d'art.* Paris, 1900

MATHEY, FRANÇOIS. *The Impressionists.* Praeger, New York, 1961

MEIER-GRAEFE, JULIUS. *Impressionisten.* P. Piper, Munich, 1907

MELLERIO, ANDRÉ. *L'Exposition de 1900 et l'Impressionnisme.* Floury, Paris, 1900

MIRBEAU, OCTAVE. *Des Artistes,* 1st series (articles appearing in 1886–96). Flammarion, Paris, 1922

MOORE, GEORGE. *Reminiscences of the Impressionist Painters.* Maunsel, Dublin, 1906

MOSER, RUTH. *L'Impressionnisme français: Peinture, littérature, musique.* Librairie Droz, Geneva, 1952

NOVOTNY, FRITZ. *Die grossen französischen Impressionisten.* Anton Schroll, Vienna, 1953

PACH, WALTER. *Renoir.* Abrams, New York, 1950

PICA, VITTORIO. *Gli Impressionisti francesi.* Istituto Italiano d'Arti Grafiche, Bergamo, 1908

PISSARRO, CAMILLE. *Letters to His Son Lucien,* edited with the assistance of Lucien Pissarro by John Rewald. Pantheon, New York, 1943

PLATTE, HANS. *Les Impressionnistes.* Paris, 1963

POGU, GUY. *Néo-Impressionnistes étrangers et influences Néo-Impressionnistes.* Paris, 1963

————. *Sommaire de technologie divisionniste: Catalogue de l'exposition Hippolyte Petitjean.* Paris, 1955

RAGGHIANTI, C. L. *Impressionismo.* Chiantore, Turin, 1947

REUTERSVÄRD, OSCAR. "The 'Violettomania' of the Impressionists." *Journal of Aesthetics and Art Criticism,* Vol. IX, No. 2, December, 1950

REWALD, JOHN. *The History of Impressionism,* rev. ed. Museum of Modern Art, New York, 1961

————. *Pissarro.* Abrams, New York, 1963

————. *Post-Impressionism, from Van Gogh to Gauguin.* Museum of Modern Art, New York, 1958

RICH, DANIEL CATTON. *Degas.* Abrams, New York, 1951

RIVIÈRE, GEORGES. *L'Impressionniste, journal d'art.* Paris, 1877

SCHAPIRO, MEYER. *Cézanne.* Abrams, New York, 1952

————. *Van Gogh.* Abrams, New York, 1950

SEITZ, WILLIAM C. *Monet.* Abrams, New York, 1960

SIGNAC, PAUL. *D'Eugène Delacroix au Néo-Impressionnisme.* Hermann, Paris, 1964

STEIN, MEIR. *Fransk Impressionisme.* Copenhagen, 1962

STOLL, ROBERT THOMAS. *La Peinture Impressionniste.* Clairefontaine, Lausanne, 1957

THON, LUISE. *Impressionismus als Kunst der Passivität.* Munich, 1927

UHDE, WILHELM. *The Impressionists.* Phaidon Press, Vienna, Oxford University Press, New York, 1937

VAUDOYER, JEAN-LOUIS. *Les Impressionnistes de Manet à Cézanne.* Nouvelles éditions françaises, Paris, 1948

VENTURI, LIONELLO. *Les Archives de l'Impressionnisme.* 2 vols. Durand-Ruel, Paris, New York, 1939

WALDMANN, EMIL. *Die Kunst des Realismus und des Impressionismus im 19. Jahrhundert.* Propyläenverlag, Berlin, 1927

WEISBACH, WERNER. *Impressionismus, ein Problem der Malerei in der Antike und Neuzeit.* 2 vols. G. Grotesche, Berlin, 1910

WILENSKI, R. H. *Modern French Painters.* Harcourt, Brace, New York, 1954

CHRONOLOGY OF EVENTS AND EXHIBITIONS

THE IMPRESSIONISTS

1857   Camille Pissarro is the first to paint at the free academy of *père* Suisse, on the Quai des Orfèvres in Paris; in the following years he will be joined by Claude Monet, Armand Guillaumin, and Cézanne.

1858   Eugène Boudin meets an eighteen-year-old painter, Claude Monet, in Le Havre, and advises the young man "to be extremely stubborn" and "to stand by the first impression, which is the good one." The two artists paint outdoors together at Rouelles.

1861   First Parisian performance of Wagner's *Tannhäuser*, at a time when Offenbach's popularity is at its height.

1862   Monet, Renoir, Sisley, and Bazille work together in Gleyre's studio.

1863   Edouard Manet's *Déjeuner sur l'herbe* creates a scandal at the Salon des Refusés. The younger generation of painters groups itself around Manet.

1864   The Goncourts publish *Renée Mauperin*, inaugurating the Impressionist style in writing, which will be more pronounced in *Manette Salomon* (1867).

1865   Manet's *Olympia* is greeted by jeers and derision at the Salon.

1866   Monet, at Chailly-en-Bière with Bazille, paints a *Déjeuner sur l'herbe* in the open air. In the following year, his *Women in the Garden* will be rejected by the Salon.

1869   Monet and Renoir each paint *La Grenouillère*. Most of the Impressionist group joins the writers meeting at the Café Guerbois, Avenue de Clichy.

1870   The Republic is proclaimed on September 4.

1871   On March 18, the government of the Paris Commune is overthrown by the army of the Thiers government.

1874   *The first exhibition of those artists soon to be known as Impressionists is held from April 15 to May 15 in the studios of Nadar the photographer (he having just vacated the premises), Boulevard des Capucines. They have organized themselves as the* Société anonyme coopérative d'artistes peintres, sculpteurs, graveurs, etc. . . . *with headquarters at 9 Rue Vincent-Compoint in the eighteenth* arrondissement.

1875   Auction of paintings by Monet, Renoir, Sisley, and Berthe Morisot, at the Hôtel Drouot, March 24. Preface to the catalogue by Philippe Burty. Prices: Monet, 165 to 325 francs; Renoir, 100 to 300; Sisley, 50 to 300; Morisot, 80 to 480.
The first performance of Bizet's *Carmen* is given at the Opéra Comique.

1876   *Second Impressionist exhibition is held in April at 11 Rue Le Peletier. The eighteen participants include* Boudin, Cals, Monet, Berthe Morisot, Camille Pissarro, Renoir, Sisley, and Degas.
Edmond Duranty publishes *La Nouvelle Peinture*, in which he defends the new aesthetic.

1877   *Third Impressionist exhibition is held in April at 6 Rue Le Peletier. Eighteen participants, notably Calsa, Cézanne, Guillaumin, Monet, Berthe Morisot, Camille Pissarro, Sisley, and Degas.*
On May 28, at the Hôtel Drouot, sale of forty-five paintings by Pissarro, Renoir, and Sisley. Prices about the same as before.
The Impressionists gather at the Café de la Nouvelle Athènes, Place Pigalle.

1878   Théodore Duret publishes *Les Peintres Impressionnistes*. The demand for their pictures is very slight.

1879   *Fourth Impressionist exhibition, April 10–May 11, 28 Avenue de l'Opéra. Among those exhibiting are Cals, Mary Cassatt, Degas, Lebourg, Monet, and Pissarro. Each of the fifteen participants makes a net profit of 439 francs.*
The publisher Gustave Charpentier launches *La Vie moderne*, a weekly in support of the new artistic and literary trends.

1880   *Fifth Impressionist exhibition, April 1–30, 10 Rue des Pyramides. Eighteen participants, including Mary Cassatt, Degas, Gauguin, Pissarro, Guillaumin, Lebourg, Berthe Morisot, and Raffaëlli.*
In June, Claude Monet holds a one-man show at the gallery of the weekly *La Vie moderne*, 7 Boulevard des Italiens. There are eighteen entries in the catalogue, preface by Théodore Duret. Among others: *Ice-floes, Winter* (1879), *Rue Montorgueil Decked with Flags* (1878).

1881   *Sixth Impressionist exhibition, April 2–May 1, 35 Boulevard des Capucines. The participants, fewer than before, include Mary Cassatt, Degas, Berthe Morisot, Pissarro, Renoir, and Sisley. Monet not represented.*
Gustave Geffroy defends the Impressionists in *La Justice*, the new journal founded by Clemenceau.

1882   *Seventh Impressionist exhibition, March 1–31, 251 Rue Saint-Honoré. Among the participants are Gauguin, Guillaumin, Claude Monet, Berthe Morisot, Camille Pissarro, Renoir, and Sisley.*

1883   Between March and June a series of one-man shows is held in an apartment at 9 Boulevard de la Madeleine, offering works by Boudin, Monet, Pissarro, Renoir, and Sisley.
Durand-Ruel organizes Impressionist exhibitions in Holland, England, Germany, and the United States.
Huysmans publishes *L'Art moderne*.
First performance of Chabrier's *España* is given at the Lamoureux concerts.

1884 The Société des XX is founded in Brussels. It will be highly receptive to contemporary art. In Paris the Société des Artistes Indépendants opens its first Salon, dispensing with both jury and awards. The "Independents" will be one of the principal showcases for the Neo-Impressionists.

Félix Fénéon becomes editor of the *Revue indépendante*.

1886 *Eighth and last Impressionist exhibition, after which the group disperses. It is held at 1 Rue Laffitte from May 15 to June 15. Among the participants are Degas, Berthe Morisot, Gauguin, Guillaumin, Mary Cassatt, Camille Pissarro, and Seurat.*

After years of difficulty, Durand-Ruel, the dealer who had backed the Impressionist movement, achieves his first success in the United States. With the American Art Association he organizes an exhibition, *The Impressionists of Paris*, which is held in New York from April 10 to May 25.

Zola publishes *L'Oeuvre*, in which at first he presents the Impressionists in a heroic light, then finally in an atmosphere of despair. Fénéon publishes *Les Impressionnistes en 1886*.

1887 An international exhibition of painting and sculpture opens at the Galerie Georges Petit, Rue de Sèze; among others shown are Monet, Pissarro, Sisley, Renoir, and Berthe Morisot.

1889 Exhibition of Impressionist painters, Galerie Durand-Ruel, Paris, April 10–20. Monet–Rodin exhibition at the Galerie Georges Petit, Rue de Sèze. Almost all aspects of Claude Monet's work are represented. Catalogue preface by Octave Mirbeau.

"Twenty years of struggle and patience," says Gustave Geffroy, who places the moment between 1887 and 1889 when the outcry against the Impressionists began to lull.

In his *Nocturnes* ("Nuages," "Fêtes," "Sirènes"), Debussy expresses his musical Impressionism. In the same year, Henri Bergson publishes his *Essai sur les données immédiates de la conscience*.

Death of Chevreul.

1890 Pissarro exhibits at Boussod et Valadon, Boulevard Montmartre.

1891 In May, Claude Monet shows his series of *Haystacks* at Durand-Ruel.

1892 Monet exhibits his *Poplar* series at the same gallery. Large retrospective exhibition of Pissarro's works; catalogue preface by Georges Lecomte. In May, Renoir has a one-man show at the same gallery, with 110 entries in the catalogue and preface by Arsène Alexandre.

1893 Durand-Ruel shows a series of landscapes by Degas; in November, a Mary Cassatt exhibition.

1894 Armand Guillaumin exhibition at Durand-Ruel.

1900 On April 14, thanks to the efforts of Roger Marx, the Impressionists are prominently and numerously represented with an entire room at the Universal Exposition. Paintings shown include fourteen by Monet, seven by Degas, eight by Sisley, seven by Pissarro, four by Berthe Morisot, three by Cézanne, as well as Gauguins, Seurats, etc. This prompts a furious outburst by Gérôme, who tries to prevent the President of the Republic from entering the room. It is the consecration.

The following exhibitions took place in the present century:

1904 *Exposition de peinture Impressionniste.* February–March. Libre esthétique, Brussels. (195 entries, catalogue preface by Octave Mirbeau.)

1905 *A selection from the pictures by Boudin, Cézanne, Degas, Manet, Monet, Morisot, Pissarro, Renoir, Sisley, exhibited by Messrs. Durand-Ruel & Sons of Paris . . .* Grafton Galleries, London.

1908 *Impressionnistes français.* October–November. Kunsthaus, Zurich.

1921 *Impressionists and Post-Impressionists.* May–September. Metropolitan Museum, New York.

1924 *Französische Impressionisten.* Galerie Flechtheim, Berlin.

1927 *French Impressionists.* Galerie Goupil, London.

1934 *French Impressionists and Post-Impressionists.* Museum of Art, Toledo.

1935 *L'Impressionnisme.* Palais des Beaux-Arts, Brussels.

1935–36 *The Master Impressionists.* November–June. Museum of Art, Baltimore.

1936 *French Master Impressionists.* October. Institute of History and Art, Albany.

Exhibition of Master Impressionists. November. Museum of Fine Arts, Washington, D.C.

1937 *Présentation des Impressionnistes* (permanent collection). Museum of Impressionism, The Louvre, Paris.

1948 *Les Impressionnistes.* Biennale, Venice.

1949 *Les Impressionnistes.* Kunsthalle, Basel.

1953 *The Impressionists.* Vancouver.

THE NEO-IMPRESSIONISTS

1892–93 *Exposition des peintres Néo-Impressionnistes.* December 2–January 8. Hôtel de Brébant, Paris.

1921 *Impressionists and Post-Impressionists.* May–September. Metropolitan Museum, New York.

1932 *Le Néo-Impressionnisme.* Galerie Braun, Rue Louis-le-Grand, Paris.

1933–34 *Seurat et ses amis.* December–January. Galerie Beaux-Arts, 126 Rue du Faubourg Saint-Honoré, Paris.

1934 *French Impressionists and Post-Impressionists.* Museum of Art, Toledo.

1936–37 *Die Divisionisten.* December–January. Boymans Museum, Rotterdam.

1942–43 *Le Néo-Impressionnisme.* December–January. Galerie de France, Rue du Faubourg Saint-Honoré, Paris.

1952 *Il Divisionismo.* Biennale, Venice. (Catalogue preface by Raymond Cogniat.)

For your special friends...

a spectacular year of REALITES *and* this limited-edition artbook

Introduce your favorite people to the international world of REALITES—a panorama of art treasures, exotic places, distinguished people, grand homes, elegant life-styles, and more.

Every other month, REALITES will explore the far corners of Europe and the Orient with the same high-quality color photographs, incomparable art reproductions, and sophisticated, informative articles you've come to enjoy as a regular subscriber.

Invite your friends to use the postage-paid cards on the flap at right to order their own subscriptions. Or, use them yourself to remember special occasions and holidays with gift subscription orders. (An attractive gift card will announce your thoughtfulness.) Enclose payment now, and we'll send a free copy of this artbook, THE IMPRESSIONISTS, while supplies last.

Share the very best the world has to offer, with a subscription to REALITES. One year (6 bimonthly issues) just $18.

If reply cards are missing, send check and order to REALITES, *132 Welsh Road, Horsham, Pennsylvania 19044.*